Lives and Times
Martin Luther King Jr.

Emma Lynch

Heinemann Library
Chicago, Illinois

© 2005 Heinemann Library
a division of Reed Elsevier Inc.
Chicago, Illinois

Customer Service 888-454-2279
Visit our website at www.heinemannlibrary.com

All rights reserved. No part of this publication may be reproduced or transmitted in any form or by any means, electronic or mechanical, including photocopying, recording, taping, or any information storage and retrieval system, without permission in writing from the Publisher.

Designed by Richard Parker and Tinstar Design Ltd (www.tinstar.co.uk)
Illustrations by Sean Victory and Jeff Edwards
Originated by Repro Multi Warna
Printed and bound in China by South China Printing Company

12 11 10
10 9 8 7 6 5

Library of Congress Cataloging-in-Publication Data
Lynch, Emma.
  Martin Luther King, Jr. / Emma Lynch.
    p. cm. -- (Lives and times)
    "Illustrated by Sean Victory and Jeff Edwards"-- T.p. verso.
    Includes bibliographical references and index.
    ISBN 978-1-4034-6351-7(library bdg.) -- ISBN 978-1-4034-6365-4 (pbk.)
    ISBN 1-4034-6351-4 (library bdg.) -- ISBN 1-4034-6365-4 (pbk.) 1. King, Martin Luther, Jr., 1929-1968--Juvenile literature. 2. African Americans--Biography--Juvenile literature. 3. Civil rights workers--United States--Biography--Juvenile literature. 4. Baptists--United States--Clergy--Biography--Juvenile literature. 5. African Americans--Civil rights--History--20th century--Juvenile literature. I. Victory, Sean. II. Edwards, Jeff. III. Title. IV. Series: Lives and times (Des Plaines, Ill.)
   E185.97.K5L96 2005
   323'.092--dc22
                        2004017434

Acknowledgments
The author and Publisher are grateful to the following for permission to reproduce copyright material:
p. 4 Getty Images/Hulton Archive; p. 6 JamesRandklev/Corbis; p. 9 Corbis; p. 10 Getty Images; pp. 11, 12, 15, 16, 18, 24 Corbis/Bettman; pp. 13, 20, 23 Flip Schulke/Corbis; pp. 14, 21, 22, 27 AP Wide World Photos; p. 17 Getty Images/Time Life Pictures; p. 25 Popperfoto; p. 26 Richard Cummins/Corbis; Page icons Hemera PhotoObjects

Cover photograph of Martin Luther King Jr. reproduced with permission of Corbis.

Photo research by Melissa Allison and Fiona Orbell

Special thanks to Rebecca Vickers for her comments in the preparation of this book.

Every effort has been made to contact copyright holders of any material reproduced in this book. Any omissions will be rectified in subsequent printings if notice is given to the Publisher.

Contents

Who Was Martin Luther King Jr.?	4
Martin's Childhood	6
Separate Schools	8
Working for the Church	10
Martin and Coretta	12
Trouble on the Buses	14
Friends and Enemies	16
Going to Prison	18
I Have a Dream …	20
A Violent Death	22
Why Is Martin Famous?	24
More About Martin	26
Fact File	28
Timeline	29
Glossary	30
Find out More	31
Index	32

Some words are shown in bold, **like this**. You can find out what they mean by looking in the glossary.

Who Was Martin Luther King Jr.?

Martin Luther King Jr. was an African-American **preacher**. He spent his life trying to make life better for African-American people.

Martin Luther King Jr. was a brave man. He was one of the greatest Americans in history.

Martin worked peacefully. He did not use **violence** to get what he wanted. He led **protest marches** and **boycotts** to fight for a better life for African Americans.

This map shows some of the places where Martin lived and worked in the United States.

Martin's Childhood

Martin Luther King Jr. was born on January 15, 1929, in Atlanta, Georgia. His father was a **minister** and his mother had been a school teacher.

Martin Luther King Jr. was born in this house.

Martin played with African-American friends and white friends.

Martin had many hobbies when he was a boy. He liked to play baseball and football. He also liked to ride his bicycle and play with kites and model planes.

Separate Schools

There were no white children at Martin's school. The **law** in the South said that children with different skin colors could not go to the same school.

Only African-American children went to Martin's school.

Martin was a very clever boy. His school grades were always good. He went to Morehouse College in Atlanta, Georgia, when he was only fifteen years old.

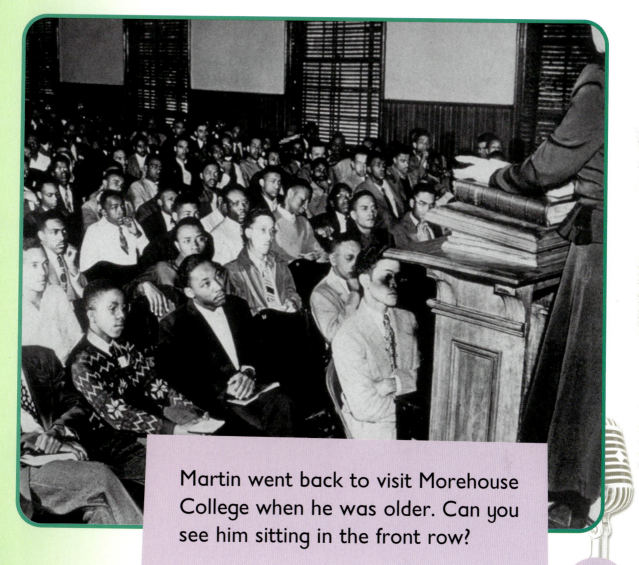

Martin went back to visit Morehouse College when he was older. Can you see him sitting in the front row?

Working for the Church

Martin wanted to be a church **minister** when he grew up. When he was seventeen years old, he gave a **sermon** in his father's church.

This is Ebenezer Baptist Church in Atlanta, Georgia. Martin gave his first sermon here.

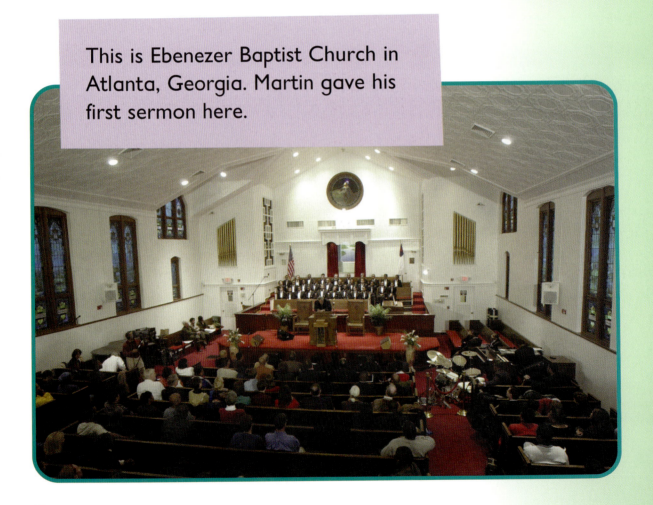

Martin learned about the work of Mohandas Gandhi. He was a famous leader in India who worked for change in peaceful ways.

Martin went to study at Crozer **Seminary** in Pennsylvania. He wanted to change the **laws** and beliefs that were unfair to African Americans.

Martin and Coretta

Martin then went on to study at Boston University. He met a woman in Boston named Coretta Scott. She was a singer.

Martin and Coretta were married in 1953.

Martin and Coretta had four children. Coretta gave up her singing job. She helped Martin with his work for the rest of his life.

Coretta still liked to sing with her children!

Trouble on the Buses

In 1955 the police **arrested** an African-American woman named Rosa Parks in Montgomery, Alabama. She would not give up her bus seat to a white man.

Rosa had broken the **law** in Montgomery. A police officer took her fingerprints.

Martin helped to **organize** a **boycott** of the buses. African Americans stopped using the buses. The bus companies lost money. In 1956 the Montgomery law was dropped.

Now African Americans could sit where they liked on buses. Can you see Martin in the second row?

Friends and Enemies

Some white people did not like the things Martin was doing. They **bombed** Martin's house to try to stop him. In 1958 a woman tried to kill him.

Martin was badly hurt, but he got better.

Martin was now famous. He gave many speeches. He visited other countries, too. In 1959 he went to India. He wanted to talk to people who had followed Gandhi.

Martin's photo was on the cover of *Time*, an important news magazine.

Going to Prison

Other African Americans joined Martin in his work for people in the South. They were prepared to break unfair **laws**.

Martin was sent to prison many times.

Martin did not stop working when he was in prison. He wrote letters to people to try to change the laws. Later he wrote a book called Stride Toward Freedom.

Martin's book was about the bus **boycott** in Montgomery.

I Have a Dream …

Martin **organized** many peaceful **protest marches**. He also gave speeches and raised a lot of money. Wherever he went, people asked him for his **autograph**.

Many people went on the protest marches.

In 1963 Martin gave a famous speech. He said, "I have a dream that one day ... little black boys and black girls will be able to join hands with little white boys and white girls as sisters and brothers."

Martin gave his famous speech in Washington, DC.

A Violent Death

In 1964 the **Civil Rights Act** was passed. It ended some of the unfair **laws** and rules for African Americans. Martin was given a special prize for his work.

Martin received the **Nobel Peace Prize** in 1964.

On April 4, 1968, Martin was shot and killed by someone who did not like what he was doing. Martin was only 39 years old. People everywhere were shocked by his death.

Martin's son put flowers on his grave.

Why Is Martin Famous?

We remember Martin for his fight against unfair **laws** and beliefs. He helped change some laws and make life better for African Americans people.

Martin showed that it was possible to change people's beliefs by protesting peacefully.

Martin Luther King Jr. was a popular and brave man. He was also a great speaker. He gave African Americans hope and belief in a better future.

Martin's life and work is remembered because it is so important to the history of the United States.

More About Martin

We can find out more about Martin Luther King Jr. by visiting the King Center. Here we can see letters, newspapers, and films about Martin's life.

The King Center is in Atlanta, Georgia.

There are many websites about Martin's life. You can find books about him in the library. Many people visit his grave in Atlanta, Georgia.

There are **memorial** statues to Martin all over the world. This one is in Westminster Abbey in London.

Fact File

- On June 5, 1955, Boston University gave Martin a special award called a "doctorate." This meant that Martin became known as "Doctor Martin Luther King Jr."

- Every year, Martin Luther King Jr. Day is celebrated on the third Monday in January. This day is close to his birthday, which was January 15.

- James Earl Ray was sent to prison for 99 years for killing Martin.

- Nearly every major city in the United States has a street or a school named after Martin Luther King Jr.

Timeline

1929 Martin Luther King Jr. is born in Atlanta, Georgia, on January 15

1948 Martin becomes a **minister**

1953 Martin marries Coretta Scott

1955 The Montgomery bus **boycott** begins

1956 Martin is sent to prison for the first time

The Montgomery bus boycott ends

1958 Martin writes *Stride Toward Freedom*

He goes to the hospital after a knife attack

1963 Martin gives his "I have a dream" speech in Washington, DC

1964 The **Civil Rights Act** is passed

Martin is given the **Nobel Peace Prize**

1968 Martin Luther King is killed in Memphis, Tennessee, on April 4

Glossary

arrested when the police take someone away to a police station

autograph when a famous person writes their name down for someone else

bomb something that blows up

boycott to protest by refusing to do or use something

Civil Rights Act law passed to make sure all people are treated fairly

law rules of a country

memorial something to remind us of people who have died

minister someone who leads people during church

Nobel Peace Prize award given to people who have worked for change in peaceful ways

organize to plan to make something happen

preacher someone who talks to people, often in church

protest marches when people walk together to complain about something they believe is unfair

seminary college where priests train

sermon speech given in church to tell people about right and wrong

violent/violence hurting people in an angry way

More Books to Read

Nobleman, Marc Tyler. *Martin Luther King Jr. Day* Minneapolis, MN: Compass Point Books, 2004.

Feinstein, Stephen. *Read About Martin Luther King Jr.* Berkeley Heights, NJ: Enslow Publishers Inc., 2004.

Places to Visit
The King Center, 449 Auburn Avenue NE, Atlanta, Georgia 30312
(404) 526-8900

Index

boycotts 5, 15, 19

Civil Rights Act 22, 29

Gandhi, Mohandas 11, 17

grave 23, 27

King, Coretta 12, 13, 29

laws 8, 11, 14, 18, 22, 24

letters 19, 26

marches 5, 20

minister 6, 10, 29

Montgomery 14, 15, 19, 29

Nobel Peace Prize 23, 29

prison 18, 29

speeches 17, 20, 21, 25, 29